Devils Tower
Giant Redwoods
Glacier Bay
Grand Canyon
Mammoth Cave

Meteor Crater
Niagara Falls
Old Faithful
Rainbow Bridge
White Sands

AMERICA'S TOP 10 NATURAL WONDERS

By
Edward Ricciuti

Published by Blackbirch Press, Inc.
260 Amity Road
Woodbridge, CT 06525

©1998 Blackbirch Press, Inc.
First Edition

Printed in the USA

10 9 8 7 6 5 4 3 2

Library of Congress Cataloging-in-Publication Data

Ricciuti, Edward R.
    America's top 10 natural wonders / by Edward Ricciuti.
        p. cm.—(America's top 10)
    Includes bibliographical references and index.
    Summary: Introduces ten unique natural formations in the United States, including
the Grand Canyon, Devils Tower, and Niagara Falls.
    ISBN 1-56711-192-0 (lib. bdg. : alk. paper)
    1. United States—Description and travel—Juvenile literature. 2. Landforms—United
States—Juvenile literature. 3. Natural monuments—United States—Juvenile literature. [1.
United States—Description and travel. 2. Landforms . 3. Natural monuments.] I. Title.
II. Series.
E169.04.R53 1998
557.3—dc21
                                                                    97–3639
                                                                    CIP
                                                                    AC

B L A C K B I R C H   P R E S S ,   I N C.
W O O D B R I D G E ,   C O N N E C T I C U T

AMERICA'S TOP

10

NATURAL WONDERS

MT

Devils Tower ★

ID   SD

WY

NE

UT   CO

Devils Tower

★ ★ ★ ★ ★ ★ ★ ★ ★ ★ ★ ★ ★ ★ ★ ★ ★

The movie *Close Encounters of the Third Kind* made the image of Devils Tower, in Wyoming, famous the world over. In the movie, the aliens landed their spaceship near this towering, 865-foot-tall rock column. Seen close up or from a distance, Devils Tower is grand, and also a little spooky, especially when the top part is surrounded by mist.

Devils Tower is the tallest rock formation of its type in America—it is even taller than most American skyscrapers. The massive rock column looms over the surrounding landscape like a pyramid built by some ancient group of giants. The Sioux called Devils Tower *Mato Tipila*, which means "bear's lodge." According to the Sioux's oral tradition, the Great Spirit built the tower to save 7 little girls from a giant bear. The vertical grooves in the rock were said to be claw marks made by the bear when it tried to reach the girls, who were at the top of the tower.

Scientists have a different explanation for how Devils Tower was created. About 53 million years ago, a solid mass of magma (liquid volcanic rock) deep within the earth was forced upward. It came to rest 2,000 feet below the surface. There, the magma cooled and split into vertical columns, which became the tower and the grooves. Erosion of the surrounding landscape eventually brought the rock tower to the earth's surface. Over time, ice in the crevices caused the stone to crack in places. Some of its columns broke off, and these massive blocks still lie in heaps at the base of Devils Tower.

Location: Wyoming
Type of wonder: Natural rock tower
Claim to fame: Tallest rock formation of its type in America
Outstanding features: Imposing size, height, flattened top
Number of visitors: 450,000 per year
Dimensions: Base 1,000 feet in diameter; top 300 feet north to south, 180 feet east to west
Fun fact: About 5,000 people climb the tower each year.

Opposite page:
Devils Tower looms over the flat Wyoming landscape.

AMERICA'S TOP

10

NATURAL WONDERS

OR

ID

Giant
Redwoods

NV

UT

Pacific Ocean

CA

AZ

MEXICO

Giant Redwoods

In 1963, the world's tallest tree was discovered on the banks of a creek in northern California by the National Geographic Society. The Tall Tree as it is called, is a coast redwood. As a group, these redwoods grow taller than any other trees on earth. When it was first found, the Tall Tree stood 368 feet above the ground—taller than a football field is long!

In 1995, the Tall Tree lost its title to a nearby redwood called the National Geographic Society Tree. This redwood was discovered at the same time as the Tall Tree, but measured only 366 feet high. It is "taller" than the Tall Tree, because silt has built up around the Tall Tree's base, which has decreased its height above the ground. Since 1995, other taller trees have been discovered and the Tall Tree now ranks 11th tallest in the world.

Coast redwoods only grow along the Pacific Coast of America, from southern Oregon to the San Francisco area. The only other living redwoods are the dawn redwood, found in China, and the Giant Sequoias, found in the Sierra Nevada Mountains. In prehistoric times, however, redwoods grew in many parts of the world. Their fossils date back 100 million years. The Tall Tree is around 600 years old and may continue to grow for many years. Although the average age of coast redwoods is 500 to 700 years, some are as old as 2,000 years.

These giant redwoods originated either from tiny seeds or from growths, called "burls," at the bases of adult trees. The two tall trees stand in California's Redwood National Park.

Location: Redwood National Park, California
Type of wonder: Giant trees
Claim to fame: Among the tallest trees on earth
Outstanding features: Towering, tapering trunks with crowns that seem to reach the sky
Number of visitors: 552,500 per year
Dimensions: The Tall Tree is 14 feet in diameter; the National Geographic Tree is 14.1 feet in diameter
Fun fact: A redwood seed is only 3 times the size of a pinhead.

Opposite page:
Coast redwoods are known for their great height.

AMERICA'S TOP

10

NATURAL WONDERS

AK   CANADA

Glacier Bay

Glacier Bay

Glacier Bay extends some 60 miles into Alaska from the Pacific Ocean. From the bay, narrow inlets that look like fingers cut into the mountainous back country. Some of the glaciers that cover these mountains reach as far as the inlets. These "tidewater" glaciers end as towering, solid walls of ice, some of which are 265 feet high. They produce immense icebergs by a process called "calving." This is believed to occur when water seeps under a glacier, melting and lifting it from the underlying rock. Pieces of the ice wall then break off. With a great rumble, the jagged chunks of ice crash into the water and float out to sea. Calving can be seen easily from the water, but for safety reasons, boats don't get too close to the massive walls of ice.

Some glaciers, such as the Johns Hopkins Glacier, are slowly moving forward into the water. Glaciers advance in shallow water, and can move up to 2 miles in 100 years. When moving forward into deeper water, glaciers bulldoze the rocks in front of them. They also melt, which makes them appear to be moving backwards. The famous Muir Glacier has retreated as much as 5 miles in 10 years. The bay's advancing glaciers originate high in the mountains—about 6,500 feet above sea level—while the retreating, or melting glaciers begin at altitudes only half as high.

Glacier Bay was established as a national monument in 1925 to protect its magnificent scenery and wildlife, which ranges from mountain goats to killer whales.

Location: Alaska
Type of wonder: Tidewater glaciers
Claim to fame: Calving of icebergs into the sea
Outstanding features: Huge ice walls, icebergs crashing into the water, mountain scenery
Number of visitors: 252,300 per year
Dimensions: The wall of the Muir Glacier is about 265 feet high (above water), and almost 2 miles wide.
Fun fact: The Muir Glacier has retreated more than 25 miles since 1890.

Opposite page:
Like a giant river of ice, this glacier dwarfs a passing cruise ship.

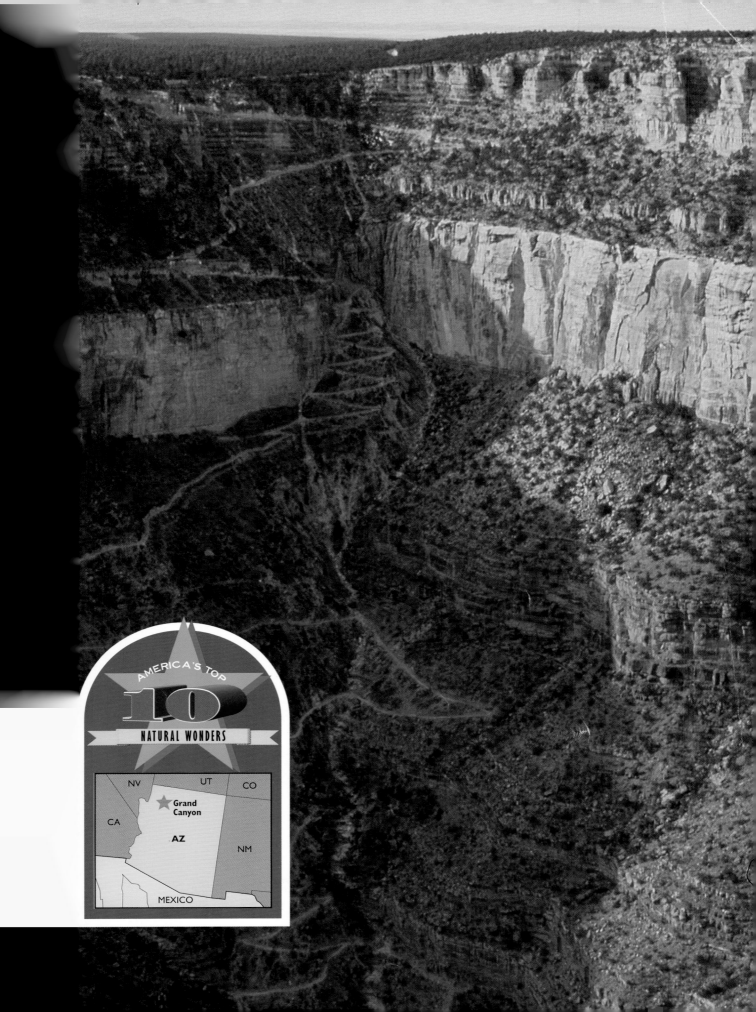

NV   UT   CO

★ Grand
  Canyon

CA

AZ

NM

MEXICO

Grand Canyon

The Grand Canyon is the world's most dramatic example of how water can erode, or wear away, the earth's surface. This place of awesome beauty, with its rugged walls of red, gray, and cream-colored rock, was carved out of the landscape by the Colorado River. The size of the canyon is monumental—277 miles long, more than 1 mile deep, and up to 18 miles wide. The South Rim is 7,000 feet high, and the North Rim rises as much as 9,000 feet from the canyon floor. Because of this change in altitude, the floor and the rim of the canyon have very different climates. On the floor of the canyon is a hot desert, while along the North Rim is a cool, wet forest. During the winter, the North Rim is blanketed by snow—as much as 200 inches.

For geologists (scientists who study the physical history of the earth), the canyon walls provide a look back in time. The rocks at the bottom are 2 billion years old. These are the remains of ancient mountains and are among the oldest exposed rocks on earth. About 600 million years ago, these mountains had been worn down to a flat plain. Fossils show that the plain was once covered by a sea and later by a desert.

The Grand Canyon as it exists today began taking shape about 10 million years ago. After the Colorado River was formed, it began flowing downhill from high in the Rocky Mountains, crossing the Colorado Plateau. Over the centuries, rocks, sand, and pebbles carried by the rushing water wore away the stone of the plateau, creating a landscape of great beauty and wonder.

Location: Arizona
Type of wonder: Rock canyon
Claim to fame: Immense size and a 2-billion-year record of earth's history
Outstanding features: Towering walls, cliffs, rocky formations, and a cross-section of the earth's surface
Number of visitors: 4.6 million per year
Dimensions: Total area is 1,904 square miles
Fun fact: Sharks' teeth that are 250 million years old have been found in the canyon's rocks.

Opposite page:
The canyon's beautiful rock layers reveal the changes that have occurred in the earth's surface over the last 2 billion years.

AMERICA'S TOP

10

NATURAL WONDERS

OH
IN
IL
WV
KY
VA
★ Mammoth
Cave
TN
NC

Mammoth Cave

★ ★ ★ ★ ★ ★ ★ ★ ★ ★ ★ ★ ★ ★ ★ ★

Kentucky's Mammoth Cave is 350 miles long. It is the longest cave system in the world. Scientists believe that not all of this vast underground world has been discovered. The cave is a maze of passages, towering rooms, and deep pits. Everywhere, beautiful formations of rock resemble waterfalls, draperies, flowers, and coral. In some places, formations called stalactites, which look like rock icicles, hang from the cave roof. Formations called stalagmites stick up from the floor.

Mammoth Cave began taking shape more than 200 million years ago. For millions of years, river and rainwater seeped into cracks in the ground, dissolving the limestone. The cracks gradually widened and enlarged to form miles of underground rooms and passages. One room, called Mammoth Dome, has a 192-foot-high ceiling! There is also a 105-foot-deep pit, known as the Bottomless Pit.

People have been visiting Mammoth Cave for thousands of years. Prehistoric tools have been found there. The first tourists began coming to the cave in 1816. Today, about half a million people visit the cave each year.

More than 130 animal species either live in or spend time within the lightless world of Mammoth Cave. Some of these creatures, such as bats and crickets, regularly leave the cave to hunt for food. Others exist in darkness and never leave. Many of these animals, like the crayfish, are eyeless and colorless. Neither feature is necessary for creatures who live in a world darker than the blackest night.

Location: Kentucky
Type of wonder: Cave
Claim to fame: World's longest cave system
Outstanding features: Beautiful rock formations, deep pits, endless passages
Number of visitors: 500,000 per year
Dimensions: 350 miles long
Fun fact: Nitrate (used to make gunpowder) was mined at Mammoth Cave during the War of 1812.

Opposite page:
Massive stalactites hang from the ceiling of Mammoth Cave.

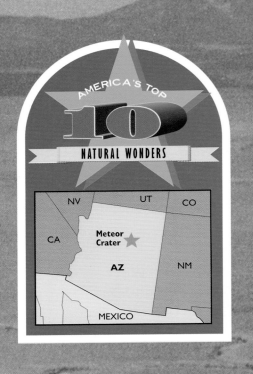

America's Top

10

NATURAL WONDERS

NV   UT   CO

CA   Meteor ★
       Crater

       AZ   NM

       MEXICO

Meteor Crater

On a desert plain in northern Arizona lies a gigantic, bowl-shaped crater. It is 4,180 feet across and 560 feet deep. Its rim rises 160 feet above the surrounding land. Originally, this huge hole was believed to be a volcanic crater. In the 1890s, however, geologists discovered pieces of iron there. Iron is a major component of meteors (masses of stone or metal from outer space that reach the earth). This fact led Daniel Barringer, a mining engineer, to propose that the crater was produced by a huge meteor. A few years later, nickel, another element of meteors, was found in the crater's underlying soil. This discovery left little doubt that the crater was caused by the impact of an object from outer space.

Scientists suspect that the meteor that landed in the Arizona desert weighed several hundred thousand tons and was 150 feet in diameter. To make such a gigantic hole, the meteor was probably traveling at a speed of about 9 miles per second. Scientists also believe that the meteor exploded when it hit the earth. The force of that explosion was probably more than 100 times that of the atomic blast in Hiroshima, Japan, during World War II. The soil on the floor of the crater contains many different minerals, such as silica. These minerals were created from the desert sand by the intense heat and force of the explosion upon impact. Scientists suspect that the collision occurred as many as 50,000 years ago. Whenever it took place, the meteor strike in the Arizona desert must have been an earth-shaking event.

Location: Arizona desert
Type of wonder: Crater formed by a meteor
Claim to fame: Monstrous size
Outstanding features: A giant, bowl-shaped hole in the earth
Number of visitors: 300,000 per year
Dimensions: 4,180 feet across; 560 feet deep
Fun fact: There are about 30 craters on the earth caused by meteors.

Opposite page:
Scientists suspect that this immense crater may have been made by a meteor that was 150 feet in diameter.

AMERICA'S TOP

10

NATURAL WONDERS

CANADA

VT ME

NH

NY MA

CT RI

Niagara
Falls

PA NJ

MD

Niagara Falls

Niagara Falls, on the border of New York State and Ontario, Canada, is considered America's most magnificent waterfall. Several American waterfalls are larger, but none are as spectacular. The average amount of water flowing down the Niagara River is 212,000 cubic feet per second. Although less than half this amount actually goes over the falls—the rest is redirected to an electrical power plant—the sound of the falling water is thunderous. In fact, the name *Niagara* comes from a Neutre Native-American word that means "thundering waters."

Niagara actually consists of 3 waterfalls. On the American side lie the American Falls and the narrow Bridal Veil Falls. These are separated by the small Luna Island. Horseshoe Falls, along the Canadian border, is separated from the American Falls by Goat Island. Together, the 2 American falls drop 190 feet and are 2,400 feet across. Horseshoe Falls is 185 feet high and 3,600 feet across.

When Niagara Falls was first formed it was only 1 falls and was located 7 miles downstream from its present site. The falls were created at the end of the last Ice Age, about 12,000 years ago. Near Lake Ontario, the river flowed over a limestone cliff and began dissolving the limestone. Eventually, the limestone caved in, and Niagara Falls was born. As the water continued to erode the cliff, the falls shifted further upstream and split into 3 falls. Scientists believe that in 25,000 years, the falls will reach Lake Erie and become rapids.

Location: Border of New York State and Canada's province of Ontario

Type of wonder: Waterfall

Claim to fame: America's largest and most powerful waterfall

Outstanding feature: Massive wall of thundering water

Number of visitors: 14–15 million per year

Dimensions: Together, the American falls are 190 feet high and 2,400 feet across; Horseshoe Falls is 185 feet high and 3,600 feet across.

Fun fact: In 1901, Annie Edson Taylor was the first person to go over Horseshoe Falls in a barrel alive.

Opposite page:
Tourists get a closer look at the thundering waters of Niagara.

AMERICA'S TOP
10
NATURAL WONDERS

Old Faithful

MT

ID

SD

WY

NE

UT

CO

★ ★ ★ ★ ★ ★ ★ ★ ★ ★ ★ ★ ★ ★ ★ ★ ★ ★ ★

Old Faithful

Old Faithful is one of the world's most famous geysers. It is one of more than 300 geysers in Yellowstone National Park, which has the largest concentration of hot springs in the world. (Geysers are a type of hot spring.) Few geysers erupt as regularly as Old Faithful, which spouts almost hourly every day of the year. This predictable behavior, along with its 130-foot-high plume of steam and spray, have contributed to the geyser's fame.

Actually, Old Faithful is not as regular as most people believe. Over the years, the interval between eruptions has varied from 32 minutes to 2 hours. Calculations show, however, that it spouts about once every hour. For many years, the average interval was 65 minutes. Little by little, this time increased to 69 minutes. After an earthquake in 1983, eruptions began occurring about every 77 minutes.

The reason why there are so many geysers and other hot springs in Yellowstone is because millions of years ago, the region experienced a large amount of volcanic activity. Molten rock accumulated below ground, and when surface water collects there, it is heated by the volcanic rock. Where there is enough pressure on the heated water, its temperature is raised above the normal boiling point, but it does not begin to evaporate. The water can reach temperatures of up to 400° Fahrenheit before it finally turns to steam. At that point it is released explosively through an opening in the earth's surface. It is this impressive and dramatic display that draws millions to Old Faithful each year.

Location: Yellowstone National Park, Wyoming
Type of wonder: Geyser
Claim to fame: Erupts almost hourly every day of the year
Outstanding features: A regularly occurring fountain of steam and hot water, over 130 feet high
Number of visitors: 3.1 million per year
Dimensions: Plume of steam and spray rises 130 feet above ground
Fun fact: Each eruption is signaled by a splash of water above Old Faithful's crater.

Opposite page:
Old Faithful erupts about once every 77 minutes, spraying water 130 feet into the air.

AMERICA'S TOP

10

NATURAL WONDERS

ID
WY
NV
UT
CO
Rainbow
Bridge
AZ

Rainbow Bridge

Tucked in a remote canyon in southeast Utah, is a huge natural sandstone bridge. Its colors include orange, red, and brown, and according to Native-American legends, the bridge was a rainbow that turned to stone. Until early in the 20th century, only Native Americans had ever seen the bridge. In 1909, they guided a group of archaeologists and geologists into the Utah canyon, and the bridge became known to the rest of the world. Rainbow Bridge is still so remote that it is hard to reach by land. Most visitors who journey there take a boat from Lake Powell, and then must hike about half a mile to reach the bridge.

Rainbow Bridge is the world's largest known natural stone bridge. It arches 290 feet above the floor of the canyon and spans a distance of 275 feet. The stone at the top of the arch is 42 feet thick and 33 feet wide and could accommodate 2 lanes of traffic!

It took millions of years for nature to build Rainbow Bridge. The process began 60 million years ago, after the Colorado Plateau was formed. Bridge Creek, which flowed over the plateau, began cutting into the surface rock, exposing the underlying sandstone. Scientists believe that the bridge was once part of a narrow rock wall that stood in the canyon. The center of the wall was slowly eroded by water. This opening in the rock gradually widened, forming the bridge. It is still being enlarged by water erosion. In 1910, the U.S. government formally established the bridge as the Rainbow Bridge National Monument.

Location: Southeast Utah
Type of wonder: Natural stone bridge
Claim to fame: World's largest natural bridge
Outstanding features: Huge span and height
Number of visitors: 346,200 per year
Dimensions: Span: 275 feet; height: 290 feet
Fun fact: The Capitol Building in Washington, D.C., could fit under the arch.

Opposite page:
The top of this massive bridge is wide enough to hold 2 lanes of traffic.

AMERICA'S TOP

10

NATURAL WONDERS

UT   CO   KS

OK

AZ

NM

TX

White
Sands

MEXICO

White Sands

★ ★ ★ ★ ★ ★ ★ ★ ★ ★ ★ ★ ★ ★ ★ ★ ★ ★

White Sands looks like a skier's paradise, with its glistening wind-swept hills of snow-white powder. This powder is not snow, however, but gypsum, a special type of sand. White Sands in southern New Mexico is the largest gypsum dune field in the world. Gypsum is a mineral that is soluble, which means that it will dissolve in water, like salt or sugar.

The dune field lies in the Tularosa Basin between the San Andreas Mountains, and the Sacramento Mountains. White Sands covers an area of 275 square miles and is separated in places by flat ground. The gypsum that forms the dunes comes from the mountains. Rainwater dissolves the gypsum and carries it down the mountains into Lake Lucero, a seasonal lake. This lake is dry most of the year. When the winds are strong and steady, they deposit gypsum grains from the lake onto the dunes of White Sands. New dunes are constantly being formed as they drift north-eastward.

The shifting sands and dry weather make it difficult for plants and animals to survive there. The soaptree yucca has adapted by spreading out its shallow roots to absorb dew from the desert's surface. Others have deep roots that tap the underlying water. Many different animals, such as coyotes and kangaroo rats, live on the edges of White Sands. Some species, such as the bleached earless lizard and the all-white Apache pocket mouse, have adapted to the unique environment. Like the sand, they are completely white.

Location: White Sands National Monument, New Mexico

Type of wonder: Sand dunes

Claim to fame: Largest deposit of gypsum on the earth's surface

Outstanding features: Vast landscape of snow-white sand, miles of shifting dunes

Number of visitors: 604,800 per year

Dimensions: About 275 square miles

Fun fact: Some of the plants growing in White Sands have 40-foot-long stems.

Opposite page:
For plants to survive in this harsh environment, they must grow faster than the sand rises, or they will be buried.

America's Top 10 Natural Wonders are not necessarily the "best," but we consider each of these wonders to be the best of its type. Below are 10 additional natural wonders.

More American Natural Wonders

Name, Location, *Description*

Quechee Gorge, Vermont. *Narrow ravine, 165 feet deep, cut by Ottauquechee River.*

Palisades Cliffs, New York and New Jersey. *14 miles of 150–530-foot-high rock cliffs along the Hudson River.*

Carlsbad Caverns National Park, New Mexico. *250-million-year-old limestone cave.*

Sleeping Bear Dunes, Michigan. *34-mile-long dunes towering 460 feet above Lake Michigan.*

Badlands National Monument, South Dakota. *Landscape of rock spires, towers, canyons, gorges.*

Scotts Bluff National Monument, Nebraska. *800-foot-high, .5-mile-long bluff over the North Platte Valley.*

Lower Falls of the Yellowstone River, Wyoming. *Drops 300 feet into the Grand Canyon.*

Petrified Forest National Park, Arizona. *Fossilized trees from the Age of the Dinosaurs.*

Bryce Canyon National Park, Utah. *Basin in limestone, shale, and sandstone containing unusual and colorful rock formations.*

Crater Lake National Park, Oregon. *Brilliant blue lake in the crater of an ancient volcano; deepest in the United States, at almost 2,000 feet.*

Glossary

altitude The vertical height or elevation of an object above the earth's surface.

asteroid One of the many small, solid objects made of rock or metal that orbits the Sun.

burl A hard, woody rounded outgrowth on a tree.

calving Here, the process by which icebergs are formed when chunks of ice break off a larger ice wall and fall into the ocean.

erosion The process of wearing away the land by the action of wind, water, or ice.

fossil The remains, impression, or trace of an animal or plant from past ages that have been preserved in the earth's crust.

glacier A large body of ice that moves slowly over land or down a mountain slope.

Ice Age A prehistoric time period when glaciers covered much of the earth's surface.

limestone A type of soft rock formed mostly from the accumulated remains of living things, such as seashells.

magma Molten, or hot, liquid rock material within the earth.

meteor A mass of stone or metal from outer space that reaches the earth.

plume A shape like a long feather.

prehistoric The time before the period of written history.

pyramid A structure or object that has a square base and 4 triangular walls that meet in a point at the top.

stalactite The deposit of a mineral substance on the roof or side of a cave or cavern that resembles an icicle.

stalagmite A mineral deposit on the floor of a cave that resembles an upside down stalactite.

Further Reading

Bryan, T. Scott. *Geysers: What They Are and How They Work.* Boulder, CO: Rinehart, Roberts Publishers, Inc., 1990.

Cork, Barbara and R. Morris. *Mysteries and Marvels of Nature.* Tulsa, OK: EDC Publishing, 1983.

Frahm, Randy. *Canyons.* Mankato, MN: Creative Education, 1994.

Goodman, Billy. *Natural Wonders and Disasters.* New York: Little, Brown and Co., 1991.

Markert, Jenny. *Glaciers and Icebergs.* Mankato, MN: Child's World, Inc., 1993.

Pearce, Q. L. *Quicksand and Other Earthly Wonders.* Morristown, NJ: Simon and Schuster, 1989.

Rigby, Susan. *Caves.* Mahwah, NJ: Troll Communications, LLC, 1993.

Vogt, Gregory L. *The Search for the Killer Asteroid.* Brookfield, CT: Millbrook Press, Inc., 1994.

Wonders of Nature Take-Along Library, 5 vols. New York: Random House, Inc., 1991.

Where to Get On-Line Information

Devils Tower	http://www.state.sd.us/tourism/devtower
Giant Redwoods	http://www.nps.gov/redw
Glacier Bay	http://www.nps.gov/glba
Grand Canyon	http://www.thecanyon.com/nps/index.htm
Mammoth Cave	http://www.nps.gov/maca
Meteor Crater	http://www.flagstaff.az.us/meteor
Niagara Falls	http://www.nfcvb.com
Old Faithful	http://www.nps.gov/yell
Rainbow Bridge	http://www.infowest.com/Utah/canyonlands/rainbow.html
White Sands	http://www.blarg.net/~lkj/gallery/white_sands.html

Index

Photo Credits

Cover and pages 2, 14, 16: PhotoDisc, Inc.; cover and pages 4, 6: David A. Harvey/© National Geographic Society; cover and pages 8, 20: National Park Service; cover and page 10: ©John W. Bova/Photo Researchers, Inc.; cover and page 12: Meteor Crater, Northern Arizona, USA; cover and page 18: John Telford/Photo courtesy of the Utah Travel Council